# POETRY ANTHOLOGY

# Poetry Anthology

## PEACE
## AND REDEMPTION &
## STRENGTH FOR AUTISM

Ian M Weller

Ian Weller Inc

# Contents

## 2
# Strength for Autism 37

First Printing, 2017

# 1

# Peace & Redemption

# Peace

Peace is rare but it can be found in many places in the world.
The primary place is in nature.

The sound of mild silence and the calming wind.
The sound of Mother Nature herself.

It is a sign of tranquility.
Nature is at peace.
Peace is in the quiet places in the world.

Not places such as caves, where noise echoes.
But the forest, wilderness, or plains where noise can be made, and none will care.
Those are the places where you can find peace in both mind and body.

The places where you can find peace
Are not in a city.
Only in nature.

# Remember Me

Take what you want,
Live as you want,
Do whatever you want when I'm gone.

All I ask of anyone I know in the end
is to remember me.

Remember who I am,
Remember my name,
Remember what I stand for.

We all have our time.
When my time comes,
All I ask of those I know is to remember me.

Remember the positives of my character,
And forget the negatives.

When my time is over,
Remember me.

# Redemption

I'm not perfect.
I've never been perfect.

Even though humans were made to be flawed,
I try to live a life of righteousness
with little success so far.

I seek redemption for something I was born with.
Redemption for being flawed.
Redemption for the darkness within me.

But how do you redeem yourself,
when the only wrong on one's soul
is bearing a dark entity?
How do you redeem yourself from that?

# The Plea

My lord,
Save us from what is to come.

We don't stand
A chance against it.

It can't be outfought,
It can't be outrun,
There is no escaping it.

We can't undo
What we've done.

There is no escaping
The coming storm.

Hear us,
Hear our final plea.

Save those
Who can be saved.

Save those
That should not suffer
From our mistakes.

Save them from
The coming Darkness

# Words Bring Light into Darkness

Words can do many things.
Some can raise us up
some can knock us down
the rest don't do much.

In certain situations
some words from certain people
can make light shine
in the darkest night.

No matter how dark it gets
words can make the dimmest light
into a great flash or torch
to light your path out of the dark.

# Never Submit

We autistic are a group of people,
scattered across the world.

Those who don't understand us
leave us out of the conversation.
We accept who we are.

Yet, they call what we have a disease,
a grand flaw.

They fear what they don't understand.
Understand this,
we have a curse and a gift that we are bound to keep.
A gift we must embrace.

We will never submit to the ones that don't understand.
We will never submit to what they want.
We will never submit to a cure.

We will be supported by our families
and by our brethren around the world.

Even if a cure is administered,
it doesn't heal the history of hurt.

# Call to Autistics

I know the feeling you got.
You feel alone and at the ledge.

Listen to me and take these words to heart.
You're not alone in this world
that doesn't want to take time to understand.

Believe me when I say most texts are out dated.
What a majority of experts know is pure bull.
Those bastards would rather lock us away.
There's a new prejudice in the USA.

To the elites, we are the new undesirables.
They don't think we stand a chance.
Time to prove these arrogant bastards wrong.

We may not have a path to follow,
so we must make our own paths.
There is not set destiny or ideal for us,
so we have to make our own.

It's not easy to do
with little to no support.
Have faith in yourself.

Never give in,
you have potential.

# Learn From My Pain: Anti-Bully Poem

You had another rough day.
Those bullies came back.

Before you leave
Listen carefully to me.

Listen to what a survivor
Of your kind of situation
Has learned from experience.

Listen and learn
From my story.
Learn from my mistakes.

First,
Tell a teacher
Or the principal
What's happening.

I never did.
I hoped
They would go away.
They didn't leave me alone.

For two long years
I had to put up
With fools
Who got kicks from

My bursts of rage.

Of course that was
Before my freshman year
Of high school.
Once I was there,

I had a guardian
In my older brother.
Even though I had
Someone who would

Help me;
Be on my side
When trouble came.

The damage was done.
The scars were made
And remain still.

Even after all these years
I hold a grudge against people
And they woke a dark voice.

Even with all the medicine I take
The dark voice still whispers to me.
Now that you've heard my story,
Try to do what I could not.

# Coward with Regrets

I sometimes
Look back on
The choices I've made.

Most of them,
I wouldn't have
Any other way.

Fate has decreed
I follow this path.

But some
I wish I could change.

I put up
A great barrier
To protect myself
From others.

I not only hid
The dark plots
Of revenge
I dreamt about.

I hid My heart
From those I admired.
Crushes I've had.

Guess I'm just
A damn coward,
When it comes to love.

I regret hiding my heart.
I'm in the field of romance,
A coward with regrets.

# Can You Love Me?

There's a part of me
That I try my best to hide.
A darker side than what you can see.

They say we all have a dark side.
My darkness is almost
A separate entity within me.
I call my darkness a Demon.

Knowing this now,
Can you love me?
Can you love a man on the brink?

Will you stand by my side
And help me remember
Who I am
As I slip and
Pulled into the darkness
Within my own mind?

If you can truthfully
Say yes to all of these questions
I'm in your debt.

I hope that my heart
And all the love I can give
Til the day I die
Will be enough to repay
What you have done for me.

# Beautiful One

I am a fool for not opening up to you.

You are one of the Greatest Beauties in the world that I know.
But I form no relationships.
I blame myself and my work ethic for not expressing myself to you.
Respect can be affordable, but relationships can end in disaster.

I'm in the process of throwing my heart away, my biggest mistake.
I don't know what to do,
take the risk and expose my love to you
or play it safe and be alone.

I wish the answer was simple.

But am I worthy of you, beautiful one?
Am I worthy of your beautiful face, body, and mind?

And if I am, will fate let me love you?
Beautiful one, my heart is yours.

# Shield

You are in my heart beautiful one,
Even though we may be far apart.

When you need someone to talk to,
I will be your vent and the one who will council you.

When the sun shines we'll be together.
When it rains or when the darkness comes after you,
I will be your shield against the rain and the darkness of the world.
I will be the shield that protects you.

If you're in trouble,
You can come to me and I will help you.
For I will be the shield that will protect you
From the rain that makes life miserable
and the darkness that curses humanity.

I will protect you to the bitter end.
To my bitter end.

# Sacrifice

Whenever you need me,
wherever you need me,
I will come and do whatever it takes
to ensure you safety and prosperity.

My lady, you may already know this,
but I will tell you many times
with all my heart behind these words.
I will sacrifice myself willingly for your well being.

I'm expendable.
Whatever hole I make in your heart,
I know it will be filled by someone else or heal in time.
For me,
you can't be replaced.

I've been through too much pain
to keep my humanity intact.
It's a mystery that my anger hasn't corrupted me yet.

Let me pay the price.
Let me take the fall.
I beg you,
if a sacrifice must be made,
let me be the sacrifice.

# Reflection

I'm looking at a mirror.
I know it's my reflection
looking back at me.

But the reflection of my eyes
trouble me to no end today.

I thought my eyes were hazel,
but they appear a dark green.

Maybe it's the morning
or something else.

Green is emotional color
representing envy and jealousy.

My brother is living a life
that brings honor.
He's in the army,
he has a wife and child.
I have nothing, again.
All I've done has been
mandatory by personal
and family standards.

The only real achievement
I can give credit to
is getting third place in a
state wide essay contest.

That glory is gone.

I feel I have nothing
to be proud of.

Family is proud,
but proud of what?
What makes them proud of me?
I have nothing.

# Angel

When will Heaven send me an angel?
An angel that will love me for who I am,
an angel that will save me from the darkness within me,
an angel that will end the internal chaos in my mind.
When will Heaven send this angel to me?

# Answers

How far must I go,
What must I do,
To find the answers that I seek?

Are they right in front of me,
Or are they hidden and I can't find them?

How do you heal the pain of a wanting heart?
How do you put a mind wrapped in chaos
into a state of peace?

How far must I go,
What must I do,
To find these answers I seek?

# World of Chaos

There is a world
that is constantly engulfed in
the flames of chaos.

Since its creation,
it has been
in a stable chaos
known as survival.

When a certain creature grew
the type of chaos changed.
It was a slow change,
took millennia for its new form
to take shape.

The chaos never ends.
When the chaos fades in one place
it erupts in another.

There are always snakes
that are igniting
the flames of chaos.

Now it appears
this world will fall apart
or its reached the peak
of it's chaotic history.

There is no peak.
If there was a peak
there would be

only silence.

Many of the creatures
hope the chaos will end soon.

The snakes always return
and the flame of chaos
doesn't just diminish instantly.

It took millennia
for the flames of chaos
to be this strong.

It takes millennia
for it to be extinguished.

# Behind These Eyes

Long ago,
I was whole and satisfied with my life.
But that time has passed,

There isn't much of
The pure hearted fool that I was.
Something took the place of the fool.

I don't know what it is.
Some say the eyes
Are a window to the soul.

Behind these eyes of mine,
There is a great fire.

A fire fueled by anger, frustration,
And a hatred of something I can't name.

I can't name it for it is too vague.
It's made of so many things.

It has a human shape,
But I feel something.

It can't be humanity,
For it has an aura,

An aura that isn't normal.
It's dark.
It feeds the fire that burns
Behind these eyes.

# Can't Be Too Late

This world will never be what I hoped for.
If I don't belong, who could've guessed?

I would leave everything behind just to feel like it's not too late.
It can't be too late for change
in both my world
and the world around me.
It can't be too late.

People who care for me say it's alright,
When something inside me says it's over
Something inside me says the only way
To be free of madness is death.

There has to be another way to relieve myself of madness.
It can't be too late.

I feel I've come too far to have it end.
It's not too late for change, it can't be too late.
I must learn to forgive and to trust again.

It can't be too late to relearn,
the concepts must still be within my grasp.
It can't be too late.

Will either my world or the world around me
find the peace I search for?

# Break a Habit

I find a place to be alone,
All assume when I am alone
I am trying to heal myself,

When I may actually be
tearing myself apart even more.

I don't want to be the enemy,
But the battle never ends.

Inside I know I am the one who is confused.
I don't know how I got this way,
And I know it's not alright,
So I must break a habit,
I must break this habit of doubt.

I will break this habit someday.
I just don't know how to break it.

One day I know,
I will break this habit of doubt
and things will start to improve.

Knowing this future,
I have to start finding a way to break this habit
I will be free of doubt and live the life I should live.

# Chapters

Listening to a song again.
It claims there is greatness in all.
'Let the Light shine' is the chorus.

I look inside myself again.
Thinking about the message
within the song.

I can see the light in me,
but it's surrounded by darkness.
An island of light in a sea of darkness.

Sound very familiar.
Oh wait, that's me.

A good person lost in the night.
My story from High School to now.
Wonder what the next chapter holds?

# The Fallen

The Fallen,
they are a large group
who can't find their way.

They don't know the truth
from the dark lies that plague them.
They don't know what to do
besides move blindly forward.
They don't know who they can turn to
when in need.

They feel they must be on their own.
They are somewhat blind
to the events around them.

All they know is what has happened,
to them and to others they know.

They feel weak and helpless,
unable to save themselves or others.

They've fallen into despair.
That's why they walk forward blindly.
They have a slight glimmer of hope,
in the center of all
their sorrow and despair.
But that glimmer is like a boat,
in the middle of the raging sea.

I know this for one reason,
I am one of the Fallen

My lord,
save the Fallen.

Save those who can't find their way.
Save those who are lost to themselves.

I do not ask for myself.
I know there are others
that are like me somewhere.
I'm certain they are just as lost as I am,
thus they are among the fallen.

I don't care about myself
as much as those who are also lost.

I can wait.
Save those that can be saved first,
then you can save me.

# Warrior's Heart

I'm ready to do what must be done.
I know what may need to be sacrificed.
Yet I dare not falter.

With a warrior's heart,
I will face the challenge
and I will overcome
no matter the cost.
Even if my life may be the price.

# Fire in My Heart

Anywhere I go,
There's always a fire near.

It roars and burns silently
And it is hidden in plain sight.

There is a fire in my heart.
A fire fueled by many things.
Ambition,
Rage,
Darkness,
To name the few I'm aware of.

My heart is growing cold,
But the fire
Is making the ice
Turn into crystals.

At the end of the process
My heart will be a crystal
Encasing the fire
That lives in my heart.

# Fight

I fight
A personal war
That I won't win.
I won't win
Fighting alone.

But I don't know
Anyone who can
Help me in this fight.

I've had people
Who have been
On my side.

But I don't have
Anyone that
Will stay by me.

I will fight
No matter the price.

I have to
Because I have
No other option.

# Invisible Key

There were keys around my neck
at one time.

The two that could be seen are minor,
Compared to the key that can't be seen.
The invisible key.

It's the key to
my art,
the key to
The source of most of my art,
The key to what I hide.

It opens the cell
that cages what I hide.
Yes,
It's the key
to the Darkness
and it is the key
to my wounded heart.

This key
is never to be touched by anyone.
I alone can use it.

It's better that way.
Trust me.
It's the only option.

# Journey

What is your goal?
What is it that you want?
If you feel that your goal or what you want is worthwhile,
go forth and claim it.

Do what you must.
Fight to the end.
Keep your eye on the prize.
Never submit.

Once you obtain it,
look back at what you've done.
From the moment you decided to the moment of glory.
Ask yourself,
"How hard was it?"

If your answer is "It was easy",
then this thing whether glory or possession,
was not as worthwhile as you thought at the beginning.

It's not the goal, the item, or the destination,
that makes something worthwhile,
it's the journey and the challenge that makes something worthwhile.

# Prayer for the Purge

My Lord,
There may be no reason for you to hear us out,
but lend us your ear for a moment.
Spare those who fight the losing fight to preserve your greatest gift.
You made this world for us and many of your other creations.

Our kind has forgotten.
We have forgotten our place.

We think with selfish minds.
Many ignore the right that your other creations have.
They should not be driven out,
for the sake of greed and easy living.

Show mercy to those who fight
to save what's left of your gift to us.

We know the purge is coming.
Few take the right path by saving what they can.
While many take the easy path,
and treat this great gift of yours as if it can be replaced.

Show mercy to those who take the right path.
And those who have taken the easy path,
do as you wish.
For they have done many wrongs.

As a whole,
we have damned ourselves.
We deserve whatever fate you decide.

# Lost Heart

Alone again,
lost within myself.

I search for something,
I think I know what it is.

I can feel its pain.
It is wounded and has hidden itself.

I'll still search for it,
even if in the end I wish I hadn't.

It's close,
I can sense it.

As I get a glance,
it disappears.

I recognized it and
understand its situation.

I was the one who wounded it,
I'm responsible for its pain.

The question is,
"How do I heal it?"

How do I heal the heart that I wounded?
What must I do to heal my own heart?

# Solemn Call

Sanctus Espiritus,
In our solemn hour
Please hear me

Hopeful am I
You will hear our cry
And forgive us.

Forgive us for
Abandoning you
And bowing to
A false entity.

Astonished by its power
When it appeared
We yielded and gave into
The false being.
Now we flee
From the Scythe
That will condemn us
To you,

The Great One we
Foolishly threw to the side.

Forgive us Great One.
Forgive us Sanctus Espiritus.

2

# Strength for Autism

# Do You Know

Do you know
what Autism is?

Do you know
it affects 1 in 68
children born worldwide.

Do you know
that when a child
is diagnosed with Autism,
a special needs family is made.

If one person has Autism
the whole family is
part of the Autism community.

Most families are devastated
when they get the diagnosis.
They lose hope when hope can be found.

Allow me to help you
on your journey of
overcoming this challenge
known as Autism

Most know nothing,
so they do nothing.
The more involved you are
the easier the process will be.

Continue on,

and be strengthened by my words.

Listen to what an
Autism success story has to say.

# Brotherhood

Wake in this world unknown,
but know that you are not alone.

I know what you're going through.
Don't let them get the best of you.
You'll make it through this.

People with our difference
have to stick together.
Keep your head up,
they will stop looking down at you.

This is not the end.
Our fight has
only just begun.

My autistic
brothers and sisters,
Their downward glance
shall be our motivation to rise.

Let us rise
in a sense of brotherhood.

When we rise,
they will see our worth.

# Be Proud

My brothers and sisters
of situation.
I know it's hard.
What I'm about to ask
may seem too much.

Be Proud,
Proud of who you are.

If someone
calls you inferior,
they don't know anything.

They don't know you,
You may have weak points,
but you also have strengths

If you are doing
the best you can,
giving it your all.

No matter the outcome,
Be proud of yourself.

Autism comes with challenges.
If you are doing your best
and refuse to give up,
That's something
to be proud of.

All we can do

is the best we can.

If you are doing your best,
you and your family
should be proud.

# Unite

I know how
you feel.

You feel alone
in this world that
doesn't want to understand.

Believe me when I say
you're not alone.

Many of those
with our difference
feel the same way.

Autism makes us feel isolated.
We feel alone,
though we are not alone.

Brothers, sisters,
let's support each other.

May we one day unite
for the cause
that involves us all.

We must stand united
for the future of Autism awareness,
the future of us.

When awareness is well known,
may we unite with others.

United as equals,
not almost equals.

# Thankful

We can't say it openly.
We aren't very social.

Our difference makes things
difficult to say.

But let me say it now,
for my autistic brothers and sisters.
Thank you.

Thank you for supporting us,
for all your help,
for spending
so much time to help us fit in.

To our parents and
our support groups,
in school or outside,
thank you.

Though we may not say it,
know we are thankful
for all that you've done.

# Only Path

For autistics,
there's only one path
we can take.

The only path
we have
is the one we make.

Some say our destiny
is to go nowhere.

They're wrong.
We make our own destiny.

We are trailblazers.
We must make real paths
for future generations.
It's time
to shape
a better tomorrow.

To shape that tomorrow
we start by following
the path
in our hearts.

Don't let others
tell you your future.
We will make
our future.

# Don't

Listen to me.

My autistic
brothers and sisters,
listen to what I have
to say.

Don't kneel
to the elites
that don't understand.

Only bow
as a polite courtesy,
depending on culture.

In the U.S.
don't bow,
kneel,
or submit to elites.

Be polite,
at least
as much as possible.

Don't listen to them
if they say
"You have no future."

They are ignorant.
They only know
what old numbers say.

You choose your future.
Before you,
is the rough of life
you have to go through.

Let my words
be the tool you use
to carve the path
of your choosing.

# Too Far

I've come a long way.
From some experts in the 90s
saying I don't stand a chance
to having a diploma and a degree.

I still have a long road
ahead of me.
There's no chance
I'm backing down now.

I've come too far
to throw away everything
I've accomplished.

My trials are just beginning.
I still have to make
the path I walk longer.

For my sake
and the sake of
future generations
with my difference.

I must press forward.
For myself,
for anyone
who would walk in my steps.

I feel there's
too much is on the line.
I've come too far to fail.

I have to plow forward
through any obstacle
in my way.

I've done
too much
to stop
now.

I've come
too far
to lose
it all.

# Rise

Don't be submissive.

Lift up your head.
Get on your feet.

We can't stay down.
We have to rise
to prove them wrong.

I won't give up.
This is our fight,
I intend to give it my all.
I'll fight to the very end.

We all got challenges
ahead of us.
We must rise to the occasion.

This isn't just for us,
the current generation.

This fight
is for the future generations.

We rise now,
or we leave this
to the next brave soul
with our difference.

# Ignorance or Acceptance

There is tension in the air.
As our numbers grow
the tension grows.

The people
who don't understand
seek to change us.
Seek to be rid of us.

We don't need to change.
They need to change,
from ignorance to acceptance.

We are not weak,
we have our own strengths.

We are not flawed,
we are unique.

I may be one individual,
but together
we are a massive sea.

Ignorance,
can't be allowed
to prevail.

The acceptance we seek
is the only way
all win in the end.

# Dream

A dream,
an ideal,
a goal.

We all have them.
Everyone has a dream.

For those of us
with Autism,
our dreams are
a driving force.

As long as we believe,
we can achieve great things.

Dream on.
Strive.

We make our dreams,
We make our destiny,
We make our goals.

# Creating Utopia

Friends, family,
brothers, sisters,
and supporters,

We know this is no paradise.
This world is all we have,
plagued by ignorance.

We can start to
remake the world
if we work together.
If we stand as one,
and fight ignorance.

We can create a place
that outshines
all cities of fable.
we can create Utopia.

When ignorance is defeated,
Utopia can
become a reality.

# Unafraid

I'm not afraid
to stand
for my group.

Anyone
who feels the same way
is welcome to join.

Join in the cause
where we have
so much to gain
and nothing to lose.

Those with courage-
to stand and face criticism
stand with me.

Others can work
behind the scenes.

Though we have
nothing to lose,
we can't afford failure.

For a better tomorrow,
the stakes are set.

We win all or nothing.
We have nothing to lose,
for we will not disappear.

# Don't Give Up on Us

Parents and supporters,
I know we make things difficult.

We don't intentionally
make your lives difficult.

The world overwhelms us.
Our meltdowns are due to
sensory and emotional overloads.

I know we are a burden
both emotionally and financially.
Raising us is not easy or cheap.

Allow me to say for us,
'We are sorry for these burdens.'

I ask, I beg
you to keep helping us.
Without your help
our chances for success
is next to none.

Please,
don't give up on us.
Though we strive for independence
we need outside help.

I beg you,
please don't give up on us.
For all our sakes

don't give up on us.

# Autism Recipe for Success

You ready for it,
well here it is.

My recipe for
success with Autism.

It's a total of
one hundred parts.

Ten parts Luck

Fifteen parts Skill

Fifteen parts Concentrated Power of Will

Twenty parts Family Support

Up to five parts Peer Support

Five to ten parts Support Structure

Five to ten parts Stubborn

Fifteen to twenty parts Dreams

Up to five parts Ambition

Add parts until you reach
one hundred, then wait.

Substitute as needed,

also keep an eye on your situation.

You can go over
One hundred,
just try not to go under.

# Force of Change

Do you ever feel
so invisible
that it seems like
no one knows you exist.

I know the feeling.
I know it well.

Listen to me
and listen well.

Those who pretend
you don't exist
or believe
you are unimportant
are ignorant.

There is a strength
inside you.

You have to discover
what this strength is
and develop it.

Keep working,
keep improving that strength.

For one day,
you can demonstrate
that strength in its best form
and all the ignorant

will be in awe.

The world is changing
and the future is in our hands.

We can be
a force of change.

# Greatness

One day,
you can be the greatest.

You can be the best
in what you do.

You'll become
a master of
an art of your choice.

Before you can
be the greatest,
you must decide.

Decide what
you wish to pursue.

Once you decide,
you must practice.

Learn the art.
Practice what you learned,
then build on your knowledge.

Always keep practicing.
Never be afraid
of experimenting with new ideas.

Keep in mind,
there is always
more to learn.

One day,
you will be a master.

One day,
they will see.

See your greatness,
see what you can do.

# Hope

I'm waking up.

I feel it
in my soul.

A power
that can make
a new era.

A force
that makes me stand
and pushes me
to face the odds.

I only have
a small amount
of this power,
this force

It seems simple,
but hard to find
in these changing times.

It can make people
heroes of a cause.

It's the power of 'Hope'.

# Overcome

We push and push,
we climb higher and higher,
yet we are never done.

It seems redundant
and sometimes pointless.

It isn't pointless,
your labors will be rewarded.

Not with currency,
with opportunity.

We are defined by
what we overcome,
not by what makes us different.

The chances you receive
will be what helps
you show what you
are fully capable of.

Your past doesn't decide
your future.

What you overcome
will decide your future.

# Voice

If they look at us
with scornful eyes
and ignorant minds,
they know nothing.

They know nothing
of our situation.

It's time
to open their minds.

Those who understand
may have to be our voice,
since at a young age
we have silent voices.

It is hard to explain
when you are a child.

I couldn't explain
when I was a child.

When we grow older,
our ability to understand
will allow us to have a voice
of our own to stand for ourselves.

# Storm

You're standing
in a dark storm.

You don't know
what to do,
but you're trying.

Listen well,
every storm
runs out of rain.

Every dark night
ends at dawn.

These hardships you face
will come and go.

So lift up your head,
and press on.

Every storm
you will face
will run out of rain.

Every dark night
you must endure
will turn to day.

After each storm
you will emerge
better than before.

You can do this
and know
you are never alone.

# Heroes Needed

In times of change,
like these days,
people need heroes.

Heroes can be
many different things.

An example,
an ideal,
or something more.

What our group needs
is a legion of
positive examples.

I am a representation
of what we can become.

I'm not perfect,
but I must admit
I'm better than nothing.

I can be one hero,
but we need many more heroes
for the new generations.

# No Need to Hide

You're scared.

You try your best
to blend.

You tend to stand out
no matter where we do.

Let me tell you
my brothers and sisters of situation;
there is no need to hide.

Our group isn't going
to shrink.

Besides,
their path
doesn't suit us.

Why should we be a part of a crowd
when we feel uncomfortable in large crowds.

We are our own group.

By showing our fortitude,
they may come to join us.

So why be a part of the "IN" crowd;
when members
may join you?

With this in mind,
do you understand?

There is no need to hide.